W9-BVB-670

ANDY,

I HOPE YOU ENJOY READING THIS

BEST REGARDS,
CHRIS

Skill *With* People

Revised Edition 2010
Les Giblin

For more information and to download the mobile application go to:
http://www.skillwithpeople.com

For larger orders email:
bulksales@skillwithpeople.com

ISBN:0-9616416-0-6

Introducing the *Skill With People* Mobile Application

Do you have skill with people? Put Les Giblin's classic guide to career success, a better social life and improved family life at your fingertips.

This how-to guide gives you quick access to common sense tips and techniques that will help you meet new people, close the deal, or dazzle the crowd.

Answer 10 questions to find out if you are people smart. Then scroll through the skills that you need to build on. Have a specific challenge you need advice on? Go to Real Life Challenges to find out how to ace the job interview or make small talk at your cousin's wedding.

Make the most out of your personal connections as taught by the master of people and sales skills. Learn to communicate with impact; influence with certainty; and listen with sensitivity.

Available now for download

Welcome

Skill with people is the most rewarding of all human talents.

Your skill with people determines the quality of your business life, your family life and your social life.

The knowledge and techniques in this book will greatly increase your skill with people.

Do use them!

I am happy to be of help to you in this vital area.

Good luck.

CONTENTS

How We Learn
(and buy)

83%   through SIGHT

11%   through HEARING

3.5% through SMELL

1.5% through TOUCH

1%   through TASTE

How We Retain Information

10% of what we READ

20% of what we HEAR

30% of what we SEE

50% of what we SEE and HEAR

70% of what we SAY AS WE TALK

90% of what we SAY AS WE DO A THING

Human Insight #3

Methods of Instruction	Recall 3 HOURS Later	Recall DAYS Later
TELLING ALONE	70%	10%
SHOWING ALONE	72%	29%
Blend of TELLING & SHOWING	85%	65%

Understanding People and Human Nature

The first step in increasing your skill in dealing with people (successful human relations) is to properly understand people and their nature.

When you have a proper understanding of human nature and people – when you know why people do the things that they do - when you know why and how people will react under certain conditions – then and only then can you become a skillful manager of people.

Understanding people and human nature simply involves recognizing people for what they are; not what you think they are, nor what you want them to be.

What are they?

PEOPLE ARE PRIMARILY INTERESTED IN THEMSELVES, NOT IN YOU!

Putting this same thought another way – the other person is 10,000 times more interested in themself than in you.

And vice versa! You are more interested in yourself than you are in any other person in the world.

Remember that people's actions are governed by self-thought and self-interest. This trait is so strong in people that the dominant thought in charity is the satisfaction or pleasure that the giver gets from giving, not the good the gift will do. That comes second!

You don't have to apologize or become embarrassed in

recognizing that human nature is self-interest. It has been that way since the beginning of time and will be that way until the end of time. We are all alike in this respect.

This knowledge that people are primarily interested in themselves, gives you the basis on which to work in your dealings with people.

It also gives you power and skill in your dealings with others. In subsequent chapters you will see how many successful techniques spring from this understanding.

It is a key of life for you to realize that people are primarily interested in themselves and not in you.

How To Skillfully Talk To People 2

When you are talking to people, pick out the most interesting subject in the world to them to talk about.

What is the most interesting subject in the world to them?

THEMSELVES!

When you talk to them about themselves they will be deeply interested and utterly fascinated. They will think well of you for doing this.

When you talk to people about themselves, you are rubbing them the right way. You are working with human nature. When you talk to people about yourself, you are rubbing them the wrong way and working against human nature.

Take these four words out of your vocabulary -

"I, me, my, mine"

For those four words, substitute one word – the most powerful word spoken by the human tongue:

"YOU"

E.g., *"This is for YOU," "YOU will benefit if YOU do this," "This will please YOUR family," "YOU get both advantages," etc.*

KEY - If YOU will give up the satisfaction YOU get from talking about YOURSELF, and that YOU get from the use of the words "I, me, my, mine," YOUR personality efficiency and YOUR influence and power will be greatly increased.

Admittedly, it is hard to do and it does take practice, but the rewards make it well worth it.

Another good way of using peoples' interest in themselves in conversation is to get them talking about themselves. You will find that people would rather talk about themselves than about any other subject.

If you will maneuver people, into talking about themselves they will like you very much. This is done by asking them questions about themselves such as:

"How is your family, John?"
"How is your son in the army doing?"
"Where is your daughter living now?"
"How long have you been with the company?"
"Is this your home town, Mrs. _____?"
"What do you think of _____, Mr. _____?"
"Is that a picture of your family?"
"Did you enjoy your trip?"
"Did your family go with you, Mary?"

Most of us are not effective with others because we keep busy thinking and talking about ourselves. The thing to remember is that it is not how you like your remarks and subject; it is how your listeners like them.

So when talking to others, talk about them. And get them talking about themselves.

That is how you can become a most interesting conversationalist!

How to Skillfully Make People Feel Important

3

The most universal trait of mankind, a trait you and everybody else has – a trait so strong that it makes people do the things that they do, good and bad – is the desire to be important, the desire to be recognized.

To be skillful in human relations, be sure to make people feel important. Remember that the more important you make people feel, the more they will respond to you.

Everybody wants to be treated as a somebody. This is the basis for the Asian habit of "saving face."

Nobody wants to be treated as a nobody, and when they are ignored or talked down to, they are being treated as just that.

Keep in mind that to the other person, they are just as important to themselves as you are to yourself. The use of this trait is one of the cornerstones of successful human relations.

Some tips on how to recognize people and make them feel important:

1. **Listen to them. (See Chapter 5, "How to Skillfully Listen to People")**

   - Listening to people is just about the best way to make them feel important.

   - Failure to listen to them makes them feel unimportant.

2. Applaud and compliment them.

- When they deserve it. It must be sincere.

- Recognition and appreciation are basic human needs.

3. Use their names as often as possible.

- Call people by their names and they will like you.

- It is much better to say, "Good morning, John/Mary" than to say, "Good morning."

4. Pause before you answer them.

- This gives them the impression you have thought over what they said and that it was worthy of thinking over.

5. Use the words - *"you"* and *"your."*

- Remember, avoid *"I, me, my, mine."*

- *"You"* and *"Your"* make them the important ones.

6. Acknowledge people who are waiting to see you.

- If they have to wait, let them know you know they are waiting. This is really treating them as a somebody.

7. Pay attention to everybody in a group.

- A group is more than one, not just a leader or spokesperson.

How to Skillfully Agree With People 4

Just about the single most important step you can take to be skillful in human relations is for you to master the Art of Being Agreeable.

Truly, this is one of the gems of wisdom of our time. Probably nothing will help you so much in your lifetime as this easy-to-do technique of being agreeable.

As long as you live, never forget that any fool can disagree with people. It takes a wise person, a shrewd person, a big person, to agree – particularly when the other person is wrong.

The Art of Being Agreeable has six parts:

1. Learn to be agreeable, to agree with people.

- Get yourself into a frame of mind, an attitude of being agreeable.

- Develop an agreeable nature. Be a naturally agreeable person.

2. Tell people when you agree with them.

- It is not enough to be agreeable with people, let people know that you agree with them.

- Nod your head "yes" and look at them when you do it and say to them, "I agree with you" or "you are right."

3. **Do not tell people when you disagree with them unless it is absolutely necessary.**

- If you can't agree with people, and many times you can't, then just don't disagree with them unless it is absolutely necessary.

- You will be amazed at how seldom this will be.

4. **Admit when you are wrong.**

- Whenever you are wrong, say so out loud – "I made a mistake," "I was wrong," etc.

- It takes a big person to do this and people admire anyone who can do it

- The average person will lie, deny or alibi.

5. **Refrain from arguing.**

- The poorest technique known in human relations is arguing. Even if you are right, don't argue.

- Nobody wins arguments or friends by arguing.

6. **Handle fighters properly.**

- Fighters want one thing – a fight.

- The best technique to handle them is to refuse to fight with them. They will sputter, fume and then look silly.

The Art of Being Agreeable –
a. People like those who agree with them.
b. People dislike those who disagree with them.
c. People don't like being disagreed with.

How to Skillfully Listen to People

5

The more listening you do, the smarter you will become, the better you will be liked, and the better conversationalist you will be.

A good listener always winds up far ahead of a good talker in people's affections. This is because a good listener always allows people to hear their favorite speakers: **themselves.**

There are few things in life which will help you more than becoming a good listener.

However, being a good listener is not an accident. There are the five rules, which make a good listener –

1. Look at the person who is talking.

- Listen with your eyes as well as your ears; keep looking as long as they are talking.

- Anybody worth listening to is worth looking at.

2. Lean toward the speaker and listen intently.

- Appear as if you don't want to miss a single word

- There is a tendency to lean toward the interesting talker and away from the not-so-interesting ones.

3. Ask questions.

- This lets the person who is talking know you are listening.

- Asking questions is a high form of flattery.

- Questions can be simple as:
  "What happened then?"
  "Then what did you do?"

4. Stick to the speakers's subject and don't interrupt.

- Don't change subjects on a person until they are finished, no matter how anxious you are to get started on a new one.

5. Use the speaker's words – "you" and "your."

- If you use "I, me, my, mine" you are switching the focus from the speaker to yourself. That is talking, not listening.

These five rules are nothing more than courtesy. Never will courtesy pay off for you so much as it will in listening.

How to Skillfully Influence People 6

The first big step to getting people to do what you want them to do is to find out what will make them do it (what they want).

When you know **what** will move them, you then know **how to** move them.

All of us are different. We like different things. We place different values on different things. Don't make the mistake of assuming that other people like what you like or are after what you are after.

Find out what they are after, what they like.

Then you can move them by telling them what they want to hear.

You simply show them how they can get what they want by doing what you want them to do.

This is the big secret of influencing people. It means hitting the target with what you say, but naturally you must know where the target is.

As an example of putting this principle to work, let's assume you are an employer and you are trying to get an engineer to come to work for you. You know that several other companies have offered this person a position.

Applying this principle, "Find Out What People Want," you would first determine just what in a position and company the engineer was looking for and what appealed to this person most.

If you found out that it was advancement opportunity, you would show how much advancement opportunity you had to offer.

If the candidate was after security, you would talk security. If further education and experience was important, you would talk about that. The point is that you would find out what the engineer wanted and then you would show how the candidate could get what he or she were after by doing what you wanted (e.g., to come to work for you).

To make this principle work from the opposite position, let's assume you are applying for a job you want very much. You would first find out the abilities, duties and responsibilities needed so that you could show them that you could fill their needs. If they need a person to handle customers over the phone, you would mention that you could (or had) handle customers over the phone. After you knew what they were looking for, you could talk the language they want to hear.

The method of Finding Out What People Want is used by asking, watching and listening to them, plus the effort on your part to find out.

How to Skillfully Convince People 7

It is human nature for people to be skeptical of you and of what you say when you are saying things that are to your own advantage.

You can eliminate much of this skepticism by going at it in a different way.

That better way is for you not to make the statement directly but to quote somebody. Let somebody else make the statement for you, even if that somebody else isn't even present.

- If you are asked if the product you sell will last a long time, you might answer, "My next door neighbor has used one for four years and it is in good condition."

  In effect, your next door neighbor is answering the question for you, even though he isn't around.

- If you were applying for a position and the prospective employer wondered if you could do the work, you would mention how well pleased your past employers have been, etc.

- If you were trying to rent your apartment and the people you were trying to rent to wondered if it was quiet you would mention that the past tenants remarked how quiet the apartment was.

Now, in all these examples, you do not answer the inquiry or question. Your next door neighbor, your past employers and your past tenants do the answering for you.

The people you are talking to will be more impressed than if you were to answer.

It's an odd thing, but people won't have the slightest doubt that what you tell them indirectly is true. Yet they will be highly skeptical if you say it yourself.

So, speak through third persons!
   Quote people.
      Relate success stories.
         Cite facts and statistics.

How to Skillfully Make Up Peoples Minds

There is more involved in getting people to say "yes" than luck, guesswork, or their whim.

Those skilled in human relations have several techniques and methods, which greatly increase the chances of people saying "yes" to them. (Getting them to say "yes" simply means getting them to do what you want them to do.)

Here are four good methods –

1. Give people REASONS to say yes to you.

- Everything in this world is done for a reason. So, when you want somebody to do something, give them a reason as to why they should do it.

- However, be sure the reasons you give them are their reasons, meaning reasons that are to their advantage and benefit.

- The wrong way would be for you to give reasons that would be to your advantage or benefit.

- In short, tell people how they will benefit by doing what you want them to do, not how you benefit.

2. Ask "yes" questions.

- When you are trying to get people to say "yes" to you, first get them into a "yes" frame of mind. This is done by asking them two or three "yes" questions.

Examples –

- "You want your family to be happy, don't you?" (Of course they do.)

- "You want the best value for your money, don't you?" (Of course they do.)

- A "yes" question is a question that can only be answered with "yes."

- The idea behind "yes" questions is that if you get people into a yes frame of mind, it makes it more likely they will say yes to you.

Be sure, however, to ask "yes" questions properly. NOD YOUR HEAD WHILE YOU ARE ASKING THE QUESTION AND BEGIN THE QUESTION WITH THE WORD "YOU."

- "You want the best product, don't you?" (Nodding your head.)

- "You do want a secure future, don't you?" (Nodding your head.)

3. Give people a choice between two yes answers.

- This simply means getting people to choose between saying yes to you one way or saying yes to you another way. Either way they chose they are saying yes to you.

- It is highly preferable not to give them a choice between a yes and a no, which happens when you ask them to do something.

- Yes means they will do it. No means they won't do it.

- The skill is to have them choose between doing what

you want one way or another way. If you want an appointment with Mr. Smith, for example, you might say:

"Would this afternoon be satisfactory, Mr. Smith, or do you prefer tomorrow morning or afternoon?" (You are giving Mr. Smith a choice of times to see you - a choice of yes answers.)

- The least effective way would be to ask for an appointment. This way you are giving him a choice between yes (you can have the appointment) and no (you can't have the appointment.)

Examples –

"Do you want the black or do you want the white?"
(Rather than, "Do you want one of these?")

"So do you want to start work tomorrow or Tuesday?"
(Rather than, "Do you want to start work?")

"Do you want this charged or do you want to pay cash?"
(Rather than, "Do you want this?")

This method won't work every time, but it will work a good deal of the time. And it will work far better than giving people a choice between saying yes and no.

4. **Expect people to say "yes" to you and let them know they are expected to say yes.**

- When you expect people to say yes to you, that is confidence. However, this goes one step further than confidence. You let them know and definitely give them the impression that they are expected to say yes.

- Almost all people start off in "Neutral" and can be led.

Many never doubt or waver doing what you want, once you let them know it is expected of them.

- This is excellent psychology and will be easy for you to practice after the first few successes.

How to Skillfully Set Peoples Moods 9

You can make nine out of ten people like you immediately!

You can make nine out of ten people courteous, cooperative and friendly in one second! (With the same magic.)

Here's how -

1. Remember that the first few seconds of any relationship usually sets the tone and spirit of it.

2. Utilize the 2nd Basic Law of Human Behavior – *People strongly tend to respond in kind to the behavior of other people.*

   (Let's shorten this to: *People respond in kind.*)

So, in the first second, that instant when you first establish eye contact before you say anything, and before you break silence – *give people your sincere smile.*

What will happen? *They will respond in kind – they will return your smile and be pleasant.*

- In every human relations act – a dealing between two persons – there is an atmosphere, a mood, a stage set.

- The skill here is for you to set the atmosphere, the mood and the stage. Either you or the other person will set it. If you are wise, you will set it to your own advantage.

- One of the tragic facts of human relations is the failure of people to realize that what they put out to other people they get right back from them.

- If you put out sunshine to people, sunshine will come back from them. Put out a blizzard to them and a blizzard is what you'll get back.

- The key lies in the timing. The smile should come before you break the silence. This sets the stage in a warm, friendly mood.

- Your tone of voice and facial expression are important, too, for they reveal your inner thoughts.

- Don't forget to start your smile the same way the professional entertainers and models do, by saying this one word to yourself:

CHEESE

It works!

How to Skillfully Praise People

10

- People do not live on bread alone!

- People need food for the spirit as well as for the body. Remember how you feel when a kind word or compliment is given you? Remember how your whole day or evening is brightened by that kind word or compliment? Remember how long the good feeling lasts?

- Well, others will react just as you do. So, say the kind word or things that people want to hear. They will love you for saying kind things; and you will feel good for having said them.

BE GENEROUS WITH YOUR PRAISE. Look for somebody and something to praise and then do it.

But –

a. The praise must be sincere.

It if isn't sincere, don't give it.

b. Praise the act, not the person.

Praising the act avoids embarrassment and confusion. It has a much more sincere ring to it. It avoids charges of favoritism, and it creates an incentive for more of the same act.

Example 1: "John, your work this past year has truly been excellent." (Rather than, "John, you are a good man.")

Example 2: "Mary, you did a splendid job on the year-end reports." (Rather than, "Mary, you are a good worker.")

Example 3: "Mr. Smith, your lawn and landscaping is simply beautiful." (Rather than, "Mr. Smith, you work hard.")

Make the praise specific – pinpoint it.

HAPPINESS FORMULA –

- Get into the habit of saying daily one kind thing to at least three different people. Then see how YOU feel for having done so!

- This is a happiness formula for YOU!

- When you see the happiness, gratitude and pleasure you bring others by doing this, YOU will feel good. There is more joy in giving than in receiving.

Try it.

How to Skillfully Critique People **11**

The key to successful critiques lies in the spirit of the critiques.

If you critique mostly to "tell the other person off," or "to give them a piece of your mind," or "to put them in their place," then you will get nothing from the critique other than the satisfaction of venting your spleen and the other person's resentment; for no one enjoys being critiqued.

However, if you are interested in corrective action – in results – you can accomplish much with your critique if you go at it in the right way. Here are some rules which will help you do just that.

The 7 Musts for Successful Criticism:

1. Criticism should be made in absolute privacy.

- There should be no doors open, no raising of the voice, nobody listening.

2. Preface criticism with a kind word or compliment.

- Create a friendly atmosphere – soften the blow. (Kiss 'em before you kick 'em.)

3. Make the criticism impersonal – criticize the act, not the person.

- It is the act that should be criticized, rather than the person.

4. Supply the answer.

- The answer means the right way. When you tell somebody what they are doing wrong, you also should tell them how to do it right.

5. Ask for cooperation, don't demand it.

- It is a fact that you will get more cooperation from people if you ask them for it than if you demand it.

- Demanding is a last resort measure.

6. One criticism per offense

- The most justified criticism is justified just ONCE.

7. Finish the criticism on a friendly note.

- Finish on a note of, "we're friends, we've solved our problems, let's work together and help each other," not on the note, "you've been told off, now get on the ball."

This is the most important rule of the seven.

How to Skillfully Thank People **12**

It is not enough for you to feel grateful and appreciative to people, you should show that gratitude and appreciation to the parties that deserve it.

This is because it is human nature for people to like and respond to those who show gratitude and appreciation. They respond by giving even more.

If you are grateful to people and if you let those people know you are grateful, almost always they will give you more the next time. If you don't show your gratitude (even if you are grateful) chances are that there won't be a next time or that you will wind up with less.

However, there is quite an Art of Saying "Thank you":

1. When you say "thank you," MEAN it.

- Be sincere when you thank people.

- People will know when you are genuinely appreciative.

- They also know when you are not sincere.

2. Say it clearly and distinctly.

- When thanking people, don't mumble, whisper or slur the words.

- Say thanks as if you are glad you are saying it.

3. Look at the people you thank.

- It means so much more when you look at the people you thank.

- Anybody worth thanking is worth looking at.

4. Thank people by name.

- Personalize your thanks by names.

- It makes a lot of difference to say, "thank you, Mary" instead of "thank you."

5. Work at thanking people.

- This means to watch for chances to show your appreciation.

- The average person will thank for the obvious - the above average person for the not so obvious.

- As simple as the above rules are, very few techniques are more important in human relations than the ability to properly thank people.

This will be a great asset to you all through your life.

How to Skillfully Make a Good Impression **13**

To a great extent we control others' opinions of us. We start off as strangers to everyone and their opinion of us is largely determined by the way we conduct ourselves. Knowing this, it behooves all of us to conduct ourselves in such a manner that the effect on other people will be good.

If you want people to think well of you, to look up to you, to look upon you with admiration and respect, you must give them the impression that you deserve that rating. This is done primarily by the value put on yourself.

Be proud of yourself (but not conceited), of who you are, of what you do, of where you work. Don't apologize for your station in life or for yourself. You are what you are, so handle yourself with pride and respect.

Example: When people ask you what you do for a living, it is very important how you answer them. Let's assume you sell insurance. Which of the following answers is stated with more pride?

"Oh, I'm just another insurance peddler."

They couldn't possibly be impressed with you, for you have told them that you weren't worth their being impressed.

Handle yourself with pride and respect.

"I'm fortunate enough to be associated with one of the finest companies in the country, the Blank Insurance Co."

You can well imagine the difference in value in the other person's mind that the second answer would get over the first answer.

Other ways to make a good impression:

1. Be sincere.

- Stay away from cheap flattery, empty promises and meaningless words.

- Say only things which you mean.

- Believe those things that you say.

2. Show enthusiasm.

- This is a priceless asset that you can acquire by just selling yourself on what you are doing.

- Enthusiasm is contagious. Only after you sell yourself, and not until, can you sell others.

3. Don't be overanxious.

- In dealing with people, avoid seeming overanxious.

- Overanxiety starts people wondering and gives them doubts.

- People have a strong tendency to balk at any action in which they feel you are overly anxious for them doing. Their instinct will be to get suspicious or to drive a harder bargain.

- Conceal your anxiety. Be an actor.

4. **Don't try to build yourself up by running other people down.**

- Always stand on your own merits; don't try to make yourself look good by making other people look bad.

- True progress in life will be determined by your own efforts and worth. You cannot get far "advancing over the bodies of others."

- Keep the emphasis on yourself. You do that when you stand on your own merits. When you run others down to make yourself look good, the emphasis is on them, not on you.

5. **Don't knock anybody or anything.**

- If you can't say something good, say nothing.

- It is wrong to knock, but that is not the main reason not to knock. The main reason is that knocks and knocking boomerang and hurt the knocker himself.

- Knocking just reveals one's inner self.

- Be shrewd, be smooth; don't knock.

How to Skillfully Make a Talk

14

Here are five rules that, if you observe them, will make you an interesting speaker. They make the difference between interesting talkers and uninteresting ones.

1. Know what you want to say.

- If you don't know exactly what you want to say, don't get on your feet or open your mouth.

- Speak with authority, from knowledge, and with confidence. This can only be if you know what you want to say.

2. Say it and sit down.

- Be brief, be to the point and then sit down.

- Remember, no one was ever criticized for saying too little. If more is desired from you, it will be asked of you.

- Quit a winner.

3. Look at the audience while you talk.

- The importance of this rule is hard to overstate. Anybody worth talking to is worth looking at.

- That is why speakers who read their speeches rarely go over.

4. Talk about what the audience is interested in.

- It is not what you want to say that is important. It is what the audience wants to hear.

- The audience's interest is paramount, not yours.

- A sure-fire method of being a winning and well-liked speaker is to tell people what they want to hear.

5. Don't try to make a speech.

- Don't try to orate – few can. Make a talk instead.

- Be natural, be yourself. That is why you are making the talk.

- Just say what you have to say, naturally.

Some Final Thoughts For You 15

Knowledge itself is of no value. It is THE USE OF KNOWLEDGE that makes it valuable. Putting this thought another way - life does not pay off for you on what you can do. Life pays off for you on what you do.

This knowledge is your key to a better life, more friends, more success and more happiness. Put this knowledge to work for you and your family NOW.

I hope you do.

Good luck!

Les

50380347R00026

Made in the USA
Charleston, SC
23 December 2015